HILLARY CLINTON

biography bio book

by David Right

PREFACE

Hillary Rodham Clinton, wife of Bill Clinton, was the United States Secretary of State and US Senator. She was the First Lady of the United States between 1993 and 2001. She chaired the Legal Services Corporation in 1978 and was the partner at Rose Law Firm the following year. She has been enlisted among the 100 most influential lawyers in America.

Hillary Clinton has ☐uite a few 'firsts' to her credit; she was the first First Lady to hold a post-graduate degree, the first First Lady to run for elected office and the first former First Lady to serve in the US Cabinet.

Table of Contents

CHAPTER 1- THE BIOGRAPHY OF HILLARY CLINTON

Hillary Clinton, in full Hillary Rodham Clinton, née Hillary Diane Rodham (born October 26, 1947, Chicago, Illinois, U.S.), American lawyer and politician who served as a U.S. senator (2001–09) and secretary of state (2009–13) in the administration of Pres. Barack Obama. She also served as first lady (1993–2001) during the administration of her husband, Bill Clinton, 42nd president of the United States. As the Democratic Party's nominee for president in 2016, she became the first woman to top the presidential ticket of a major party in the United States.

Early Life

The first president's wife born after World War II, Hillary was the eldest child of Hugh and Dorothy Rodham. She grew up in Park Ridge, Illinois, a Chicago suburb, where her father's textile business provided the family with a comfortable income; her parents' emphasis on hard work and academic excellence set high standards.

A student leader in public schools, she was active in youth programs at the First United Methodist Church. Although she later became associated with liberal causes, during this time she adhered to the Republican Party of her parents. She campaigned for Republican presidential candidate Barry Goldwater in 1964 and chaired the local chapter of the Young Republicans. A year later, after she enrolled at Wellesley College, her political views began to change. Influenced by the assassinations of Malcolm X, Robert F. Kennedy, and Martin Luther King

Jr., she joined the Democratic Party and volunteered in the presidential campaign of antiwar candidate Eugene McCarthy.

After her graduation from Wellesley in 1969, Hillary entered Yale Law School, where she came under the influence of Yale alumna Marian Wright Edelman, a lawyer and children's rights advocate. Through her work with Edelman, she developed a strong interest in family law and issues affecting children.

Religious Affiliation:

Methodist. In being raised within the original tenets of Methodism as preached by its founder, John Wesley, Hillary Clinton's faith inculcated her with a sense of duty towards not just those in need in her community but also those in the world at large. She was baptized in the parish of her paternal ancestors, the Court Street Methodist Church in Scranton, Pennsylvania.

In 1961, her First United Methodist Church of Park Ridge's youth group was led by a new youth minister, Don Jones, who introduced the students to the "University of Life," that encouraged them into social action as a way of enacting the Methodist ideology. Jones would lead the group outside the comfort zone of their middle-class, white suburban neighborhood into areas of need and where they found ways to volunteer in community service. Discussions on matters of racial e☐uality and social justice permanently altered her consciousness about the larger world and the problems within it.

Education:

Eugene Field Elementary School, Park Ridge, Illinois, 1953-1957.

In grade school, Hillary Rodham was an eager student lucky to have attentive and imaginative teachers, and she wrote an autobiography and co-wrote and produced a play about an imaginary trip to Europe. She also won her first "election" in these years, as a co-captain of the safety patrol.

Ralph Waldo Emerson Middle School, Park Ridge, Illinois, 1957-1961

Maine Township High School, East and South, Park Ridge, 1961-1965

In high school, Hillary Rodham was as immersed as her peers in popular culture, heading up a fan club for the singer Fabian, crushing on one of the Beatles and attending a Rolling Stones concert.

She also succeeded academically, becoming a National Honor Society member, joining a debating society, and being elected to student council and as the junior class vice president. She later reflected on how influential Paul Carlson, her ninth-grade history teacher had been on her thinking about individualism and the rights of each person to determine their own fate, in the context of that era's anti-communism that was a large part of the agenda of the conservative wing of the Republican Party.

As part of an effort to create greater understanding among divisive sub-groups within her high school, she was asked by the principal to serve on a "Cultural Values Committee." The group's efforts to find common bonds among the disparate student body was her first recognition of what she would come to identity as the crucial "American value" of "pluralism," the idea that however different the details of their acculturation, all Americans were united by a set of values, most important among them being "mutual respect and understanding." Her work on the committee led to her first appearance on television to discuss their work.

As Senior Class president, Hillary Clinton became the first student speaker at graduation, addressing the audience of faculty, graduates, their families, and guests in a speech that made national news.

Lawyer And First Lady Of Arkansas

Although Hillary met Bill Clinton at Yale, they took separate paths after graduation in 1973. He returned to his native Arkansas, and she worked with Edelman in Massachusetts for the Children's Defense Fund. In 1974 Hillary participated in the Watergate in□uiry into the possible impeachment of Pres. Richard M. Nixon. When her assignment ended with Nixon's resignation in August 1974, she made what some people consider the crucial decision of her life—she moved to Arkansas. She taught at the University of Arkansas School of Law, and, following her marriage to Bill Clinton on October 11, 1975, she joined the prominent Rose Law Firm in Little Rock, Arkansas, where she later became a partner.

After Bill was elected governor of Arkansas in 1978, she continued to pursue her career and retained her maiden name (until 1982), bringing considerable criticism from voters who felt that her failure to change her name indicated a lack of commitment to her husband. Their only child, Chelsea Victoria, was born in 1980.

Throughout Bill's tenure as governor (1979–81, 1983–92), Hillary worked on programs that aided children and the disadvantaged; she also maintained a successful law practice. She served on the boards of several high-profile corporations and was twice named one of the nation's 100 most influential lawyers (1988, 1991) by the National Law Journal. She also served as chair of the Arkansas Education Standards Committee and founded the Arkansas Advocates for Children and Families. She was named Arkansas Woman of the Year in 1983 and Arkansas Young Mother of the Year in 1984.

First Lady Of The United States

With a professional career une☐ualed by any previous presidential candidate's wife, Hillary was heavily scrutinized. Conservatives complained that she had her own agenda, because she had worked for some liberal causes. During one campaign stop, she defended herself from such criticism by asserting that she could have "stayed home and baked cookies." This impromptu remark was picked up by the press and used by her critics as evidence of her lack of respect for women who are full-time homemakers.

Some of Hillary's financial dealings raised suspicions of impropriety and led to major investigations after she became the first lady. Her investment in Whitewater, a real estate development in Arkansas, and her commodities trading in 1978–79—through which she reportedly turned a $1,000 investment into $100,000 in a few months—came under close scrutiny.

During the 1992 campaign, Bill Clinton sometimes spoke of a "twofer" ("two for the price of one") presidency, implying that Hillary would play an important role in his administration. Early indications from the Clinton White House supported this interpretation. She appointed an experienced staff and set up her own office in the West Wing, an

9

unprecedented move. Her husband appointed her to head the Task Force on National Health Care, a centerpiece of his legislative agenda. She encountered sharp criticism when she closed the sessions of the task force to the public, and doctors and other health care professionals objected that she was not a "government official" and had no right to bar them from the proceedings. An appeals court later supported her stand, ruling that presidents' wives have a long-standing "tradition of public service" acting "as advisers and personal representatives of their husbands." To promote the findings of the task force, she appeared before five congressional committees and received considerable and mostly favourable press coverage for her expertise on the subject. But Congress ultimately rejected the task force's recommendations, and her role in the health care debate galvanized conservatives and helped Republicans recapture Congress in the 1994 elections

Hillary was criticized on other matters as well, including her role in the firing of seven staff members from the White House travel office ("Travelgate") and her involvement in legal maneuvering by the White House during the Whitewater investigation. As the 1996 election approached, she was less visible and played a more traditional role as first lady. Her first book, It Takes a Village: And Other Lessons Children Teach Us (1996), described her views on child rearing and prompted accolades from supporters and stark criticism from her opponents.

Revelations about President Clinton's affair with White House intern Monica Lewinsky brought the first lady back into the spotlight in a complex way. She stood faithfully by her husband during the scandal—in which her husband first denied and then admitted to having had a sexual relationship with Lewinsky—and throughout his ensuing impeachment and trial in the Senate.

In 1999 Hillary Rodham Clinton made history of a different sort when she launched her candidacy for the U.S. Senate seat from New York being vacated by Daniel Patrick Moynihan. To meet the state's residency reuirement, she moved out of Washington, D.C., on January 5, 2000, to a house that she and the president purchased in Chappaua, New York. After a bitter campaign, she defeated Republican Rick Lazio by a substantial margin to become the first first lady to win elective office. Although often a subject of controversy, Hillary showed that the ceremonial parts of the first lady's job could be merged with a strong role in public policy and that the clout of the first lady could be converted into a personal political power base.

CHAPTER 2- HILLARY CLINTON OCCUPATION BEFORE AND AFTER MARRIAGE

Marriage:

27 years old, married 1975, October 11, Fayetteville, Arkansas to William Jefferson "Bill" Clinton (born August 19, 1946, Hope, Arkansas), professor of law.

Although her education, legal and professional experience led to her being given a number of choices at well-paying and established New York and Washington law firms, she decided to instead "follow my heart" and go to the small-town of Fayetteville, Arkansas where her boyfriend Bill Clinton was working as a law professor at the University of Arkansas Law School. Hillary Rodham also joined the law school faculty there as assistant professor of law.

While they were dating, Bill Clinton secretly purchased a small house in Fayetteville that she had noticed and remarked that she had liked. When he proposed marriage to her and she accepted, he revealed that they owned the house. Their modest wedding ceremony and reception were held in their new home. The Clinton home in Fayetteville is now a museum.

They married and lived there, briefly. Following Bill Clinton's election in 1976 as state attorney general, the couple relocated to the state capital of Little Rock, Arkansas.

In 1976, the newly married Hillary Clinton attended that year's Democratic National Convention in New York, which nominated Jimmy

Carter as the party's presidential candidate. Carter asked Bill Clinton to head his campaign in Arkansas and asked Hillary Clinton to work as field coordinator in Indiana. After the couple took a two week vacation in Europe, she relocated to Indianapolis to work for Carter's campaign.

Children:

Chelsea Clinton as a toddler.

One daughter; Chelsea Victoria Clinton

(born 1980, February 27)

Hillary clinton stood up for her decision to stick with Bill Clinton, even after his public indiscretions.

'People will say, "they have an arrangement,"' Clinton told the co-hosts of the gossip often whispered about her relationship with the ex-president. 'Yeah, it's called a marriage,' she shot back, being awarded with laughs.

The former Democratic nominee writes a good bit about her life with Bill in What Happened, the book she wrote, and laid out the same case for staying together for 41 years on TV.

'There have been a lot more happy days than sad or angry days and I am very proud and grateful that I am married to my best friend, that he has been my biggest source of encouragement and support over all the years,' Clinton said. 'Many more than some of you have been alive, that we've been together.'

Occupation before Marriage:

At the age of three years old, Hillary moved with her parents from their downtown Chicago apartment to a home in the booming, postwar suburb of Park Ridge. She was an active child, joining the Brownies and Girl Scouts, a girl's baseball team, and was often out biking, swimming and skating.

Even as a young girl, much of the diligence she would show later in her professional life were in evidence. In 1959, she organized backyard carnivals, sport competitions and gaming contests to raise money to raise funds, by nickels and dimes, on behalf of a local United Way campaign. It led to her first bit of publicity, appearing in a local newspaper photograph with other children handing over a paper bag of the money they raised. Hillary Rodham also worked as a babysitter both after school and during her vacation breaks, sometimes watching the children of migrant Mexicans brought to the Chicago area for itinerant work.

Ambitious at one point to become an astronaut, she wrote to NASA and received a response that stunned her when she was informed that women were not accepted for the astronaut program.

Influenced by her father's strong loyalty to the Republican Party, Hillary Rodham was active in a young Republican group. She actively campaigned for Republican presidential candidate Barry Goldwater in 1964. Also influenced by her mother, who was a Democratic, she was inspired to work in some form of public service after hearing a speech in Chicago by Reverend Martin Luther King.

In the summer of 1968, she was accepted into the Wellesley Internship Program in Washington, for nine weeks, assigned to work as an intern for the House Republican Conference. In that capacity, she was directly led by the future US President Gerald Ford, then serving as House

Minority Leader, as well as congressmen Melvin Laird of Michigan and Charles Goodell of New York.

She was then invited by Goodell to continue working as an intern on behalf of New York Governor Nelson Rockefeller's last-minute presidential bid at the 1968 Republican National Convention in Miami, Florida. She attended the convention and watched as Richard Nixon was nominated for the presidency by his party.

In her senior year, she researched and wrote a thesis on Chicago community organizer Saul Alinsky. Although she agreed with his premise that the disadvantaged of society had to be empowered to help themselves, she did not agree that social change came about best from working outside the establishment but rather from within. Although he offered her a chance to work with him after she graduated, Hillary Rodham decided instead to attend law school and work from within the system.

She also worked at various jobs during her summers as a college student. In 1969, for example, she spent the summer washing dishes at a Denali National Park restaurant and sliming and boxing salmons in a canning factory in Valdez, Alaska fish factory.

In 1970, she secured a grant and first went to work for what would become the Children's Defense Fund. Part of her research work that summer involved the concurrent Senate hearings held by Senator Walter Mondale's (Minnesota Democrat) subcommittee on migrant workers, researching migrant problems in housing, sanitation, health, and education. Upon her return to Yale Law School, Miss Rodham determined to commit her focus to studying the law and how it affected children.

On the final day of her law classes in the spring of 1971, she met fellow law student Bill Clinton from Arkansas and had their first date by going to the Yale Art Gallery to see a Mark Rothko exhibit. In the summer of 1971, Hillary Rodham worked as a clerk at the small law form Treuhaft, Walker and Burnstein in Oakland, California. Bill Clinton, already declaring his love for her, followed Hillary Rodham and they lived in Berkeley, near the University of California campus.

Upon graduation from law school, she served as staff attorney for the Children's Defense Fund in Cambridge, Massachusetts. In the summer of 1972, however, she joined Bill Clinton, living in a series of western states working for the Democratic presidential candidate George McGovern's campaign.

In 1973 and 1974, while simultaneously working at the New Haven Legal Services during her post-graduate year at the Yale Child Study Center, she became exposed to severe cases of child neglect and abuse. The convergence of this work led her to help draft the legal process that the medical staff of the Yale-New Haven Hospital would use in dealing with cases where child abuse was suspected.

Hillary Rodham's first published scholarly article, "Children Under the Law" was published in the Harvard Educational Review in 1974. The article explored the sensitive issues involving to what degree judicial and legal powers should intervene in cases of child abuse and neglect.

In the spring of 1974, she returned to Washington as a member of the presidential impeachment in□uiry staff advising the Judiciary Committee of the House of Representatives during the Watergate Scandal.

With Nixon's resignation in August of that year, the need for the continued work ceased.

Occupation after Marriage

A year after her marriage, Hillary Clinton, retaining her maiden name for work, accepted an offer to join the Rose Law Firm in Little Rock, Arkansas becoming the old, established firm's first woman partner. In 1979, she became a full partner at the Rose Law Firm. She was twice named to the list of "The 100 Most Influential Lawyers in America." She also represented and later served on the board of Arkansas businesses including TCBY ("The Country's Best Yoghurt"), and Wal-Mart.

In 1978, Bill Clinton was elected to the first of five of non-consecutive terms as Governor of Arkansas and Hillary Clinton, while retaining her job as an attorney, became the state's First Lady. Shortly after the gubernatorial inauguration, she granted a local television interview about her new life.

Finding a balance between the expected concessions to a far more traditional woman's role as the spouse of a governor in a southern state, yet remain genuine in terms of her own professional interests and pursuits was a difficult challenge for Hillary. She ceased using her maiden name exclusively.

Along with her public duties, work as an attorney, wife and mother, in 1978, she also assumed a further public commitment, accepting the offer of President Carter of appointment to the Legal Services Corporation.

As First Lady of Arkansas for twelve years, she chaired the Arkansas Educational Standards Committee, conducting county studies on teacher performance and student testing, and offering recommendations for overhauling the state system.

While the state's first lady, she also co-founded the Arkansas Advocates for Children and Families, and served on the boards of the Arkansas Children's Hospital, Legal Services, and the Children's Defense Fund. Mrs. Clinton wrote a weekly newspaper column entitled "Talking It Over."

CHAPTER 3- HILLARY CLINTON AND THE PRESIDENTIAL NOMINEE

Hillary Clinton was the 2016 Democratic nominee for president of the United States. She conceded the race on November 9, 2016, to Donald Trump. She declared her candidacy on April 12, 2015, and officially received the nomination of the Democratic Party on July 26, 2016, at the Democratic National Convention.

Clinton had been on the national political stage since 1991 when her husband, then-Governor of Arkansas Bill Clinton (D), launched his presidential campaign, eventually defeating sitting President George H.W. Bush (R) in the general election in November 1992. Clinton was a politically active first lady focused on children's welfare and women's issues. During Bill Clinton's first term in the White House, Hillary Clinton spearheaded an unsuccessful effort to establish universal healthcare coverage in the U.S. She also advocated for the Children's Health Insurance Program and the Adoption and Safe Families Act.

In 2000, Clinton ran a successful campaign for the U.S. Senate in New York, becoming the only first lady to win an elective office. She served on the Senate Armed Services Committe, worked to secure billions in emergency funds for New York in the wake of the September 11 terrorist attacks, and backed a resolution to authorize military force in Ira□ in 2002. Clinton won a second term in the Senate in 2006 by a margin of 36 percentage points.

Clinton launched her first presidential campaign on January 20, 2007. In the early months of the Democratic primary, she led then-Sens.

Barack Obama (Ill.) and John Edwards (S.C.) in national polls, but was narrowly defeated by Obama after key losses in states like Iowa and North Carolina. In her concession speech on June 8, 2008, Clinton noted the historic nature of her performance, "Although we were not able to shatter that highest and hardest glass ceiling this time, thanks to you it has 18 million cracks in it."

A month after Obama won the general election, he announced that Clinton would serve in his cabinet as secretary of state. While acting as the nation's top diplomat from 2009 to 2013, Clinton used a private email server to conduct official state business, raising ⬜uestions about her compliance with government regulations on record-keeping and security that have followed her throughout her second presidential run.

Clinton formally received the Democratic Party's presidential nomination on July 26, 2016, after defeating U.S. Sen. Bernie Sanders (I-Vt.) in a closely contested primary. In doing so, she became the first woman to be nominated for president by a major political party in the United States.

Domestic campaign

Including her time as first lady of Arkansas and of the nation, Hillary Clinton has spent 31 years in government life. So it's little wonder that she tends to talk about her presidency in terms of policy-heavy proposals compared with her opponent, businessman Donald J. Trump, who has never worked in government.

Clinton's website has nearly 40 pages outlining policy positions plus additional fact sheets for every proposal. Trump, the billionaire who prefers to offer his ideas and vision with broad strokes, has a website with policies, too: It's seven pages.

"Now, I confess, I confess, it's true I can be a little wonky," Clinton said in a June 27 speech. "But I have this old-fashioned idea: If you're running for president, you should say what you want to do and how you will get it done."

Clinton's long and broad list of proposals tend to be incremental, offering modest improvements on the domestic policies of President Barack Obama. Her foreign policy and national security platform largely follows Obama's trajectory as well, which she helped steer as his first secretary of state. All this makes it hard to find a defining feature of Clinton's agenda.

"She is well informed, has thought through and wrestled with a large number of issues and policy ideas, but arguably at the expense of having a big-picture orientation," said Mark Peterson, a public policy professor at the University of California, Los Angeles.

I dug through Clinton's hefty platform and identified 10 campaign promises that we think best define her bid for the presidency. For many of her promises, though, she needed the cooperation from Congress.

1. "For families making less than $125,000 a year, we will eliminate tuition" for in-state students at public colleges.

Early on in the campaign, Clinton advocated for free tuition at community colleges. She unveiled this expanded plan as an olive branch to supporters of Sen. Bernie Sanders who favored his proposal for free public college across the board. Clinton's plan would work by providing grants to the colleges.

This plan is expensive. The campaign predicts her full higher education proposal, which includes some additional debt-relief programs, will cost $350 billion over 10 years, which she plans to cover by closing tax loopholes for wealthy Americans.

Beyond the cost barrier, Clinton would have to surmount political opposition in Congress and among state governing bodies. Also, figuring out how this would play out at each individual school would be a huge challenge, said Barmak Nassirian, director of federal relations and policy analysis at the American Association of State Colleges and Universities.

2. "Pass comprehensive immigration reform with a path to citizenship that keeps families together."

While Trump opened his campaign with a promise to build a wall along the U.S.-Mexico border, Clinton started hers with a call to "offer hard-working, law-abiding immigrant families a path to citizenship."

Throughout the campaign, she said she will push for "comprehensive immigration reform" — a package that includes a path to citizenship, increasing immigration enforcement and liberalizing future immigration.

Congress has been trying to pass comprehensive immigration reform for years. Beyond the legislative hurdle, if elected, Clinton may face additional barriers to enacting immigration policy changes from the Oval Office. Earlier this year, the Supreme Court blocked some of

Obama's executive actions on immigration attempting to give legal protection to certain categories of illegal immigrants.

3. "Stand up to Republican-led attacks on this landmark (health care) law—and build on its success to bring the promise of affordable health care to more people and make a 'public option' possible."

In the early 1990s, Clinton, as first lady, led the White House's push for a universal health care program. That effort failed amid a massive public relations campaign from the program's opponents. This time around, instead of advocating for a massive overhaul of the country's health system — which is what Sanders wanted — Clinton wants to build on Obama's Affordable Care Act and "advance toward the goal of universal health care."

Her plan involves establishing a "public option," which would be an optional government-run insurance plan. Obama and many Democrats wanted Obamacare to include a public option in the first place, but congressional opposition and the insurance industry kept it out of the law. She would likely need a Congress that's even further left-leaning than what Obama had in his first term to accomplish this goal.

4. "We will do everything we can to overturn Citizens United."

Clinton has said she will address campaign finance reform in her first months in office, specifically working against Citizens United, the landmark Supreme Court decision that allowed unlimited super PAC spending. She has also said it would be a litmus test for her for any Supreme Court nominees.

Undoing Citizens United — shorthand for campaign finance reform in general — is something politicians on both sides of the aisle have endorsed. Trump himself has railed against super PACs and money in politics. Clinton has said she would consider a constitutional amendment to make this happen.

For most times, Clinton is taking advantage of the campaign finance laws as they were. The Center for Public Integrity has noted that despite Clinton's calls to address money in politics, anonymous donors have funnelled millions into numerous groups backing her nomination.

5. "Fighting for e□ual pay."

Clinton has embraced her role as the first female nominee for president from a major political party. In most of her campaign speeches, she recites this line: "Now Donald Trump can accuse me of playing the woman card all he wants, but if fighting for e□ual pay and affordable childcare and paid family leave is playing the woman card, then deal me in."

On the subject of closing the pay gap for men and women, Clinton is advocating for the Paycheck Fairness Act, which attempts to make it easier for individuals to challenge sex-based pay discrimination. Clinton introduced a version of this bill as a senator in 2007.

This bill could make a difference for people who experience illegal pay discrimination, but it won't close the gap completely, said Jean Kimmel, an economics professor at Western Michigan University. This is because the pay discrepancy between men and women is due to numerous factors including college major, occupation and une□ual division of housework and childrearing; it's not just a problem of unequal pay for equal work.

6. "I will not raise middle-class taxes."

Clinton has a plan to take in more tax revenue, but she has said repeatedly that she will not raise taxes on the middle class. Clinton's tax plan largely keeps the tax code as is, but she says she would hike taxes for the ultra-wealthy, for example by enacting a 4 percent surcharge on incomes over $5 million and raising certain capital gains tax rates.

The nonpartisan Tax Policy Center found that tax revenue would increase by an estimated $1.1 trillion over the next decade under Clinton's plan. It also accomplishes her goal of not increasing taxes on the middle class.

"Nearly all of the tax increases would fall on the top 1 percent," the Tax Policy Center report said. "The bottom 95 percent of taxpayers would see little or no change in their taxes."

The free market-oriented Tax Foundation's analysis estimated the revenue increase to be closer to $500 billion over 10 years. The report also found, though, that ultra-wealthy individuals would see the largest dip in after-tax income under Clinton's plan, while most income brackets would feel minimal effects.

Congress has struggled to pass tax reform since the last big overhaul under President Ronald Reagan, despite regular calls for reform.

7. "Say no to attacks on working families and no to bad trade deals and unfair trade practices, including the Trans-Pacific Partnership."

Clinton's denouncement of the Trans-Pacific Partnership is one of few examples of her distancing herself from the Obama administration. While she was secretary of state under Obama, she called the trade deal the "gold standard," but in the campaign, she has said "the bar here is very high and, based on what I have seen, I don't believe this agreement has met it."

The Trans-Pacific Partnership is still awaiting a vote in Congress for final ratification. Trump also opposes the trade deal, so if Congress doesn't vote on ratification in 2016, the next president could easily derail it.

Over the course of her political career, Clinton has supported more trade deals than she's opposed, and she is generally in favor of free trade. As president, Clinton says she would "say 'no' to new trade agreements unless they create American jobs, raise wages, and improve our national security."

"We're going to increase the federal minimum wage."

Clinton says she supports increasing the minimum wage from $7.25 to $12 an hour nationwide. But usually in her campaign stump speeches, Clinton does not name a specific amount.

When Sanders was in the campaign, he distinguished himself by calling for a $15 an hour wage, and now the 2016 Democratic Party platform (to be finalized at the Democratic National Convention) calls for the same.

Clinton herself has also shown support for the Fight for $15 campaign that pushes for higher minimums in individual states and cities, and in June 2015 she spoke with a gathering of Fight for $15 members via phone and told them she supported their campaign.

Again, raising the minimum wage would re□uire action from Congress.

9. "As president, Hillary will expand background checks to more gun sales."

The national debate over gun violence has been particularly prominent throughout the election, and Clinton has made that a focal point of her campaign. She has pledged to close "the gun show loophole, close the online loophole," and "go after what's called the Charleston loophole." All three are aspects of current federal gun laws that allow people in specific situations to purchase guns without undergoing some sort of background check.

Although she has been a long-time advocate for more stringent gun control, "Hillary's position on guns are fairly standard for a Democrat," said Jim Kessler, senior vice president for policy at left-leaning think tank Third Way.

He said her proposals are in line with what the pro-gun control advocacy groups have pushed for for years, and they do not offer any sort of compromises to make pro-gun groups like the National Rifle Association any more likely to support her or her proposals.

10. "Clinton would increase federal infrastructure funding by $275 billion over a five-year period."

Clinton's infrastructure plan is part of her pledge to "make the biggest investment in new, good-paying jobs since World War II" within her first 100 days. Most of the spending, $250 billion, would go toward direct infrastructure investments — things like maintaining airports, bridges and highways — while the remaining $25 billion would fund an infrastructure bank, which would bring in private capital for public works.

Jared Bernstein, senior fellow at the Center on Budget and Policy Priorities, has noted that the plan likely won't be enough to fix the country's infrastructure problems, given that the American Society of Civil Engineers estimates there will be a $1.6 trillion infrastructure funding gap by 2020.

Bernstein also pointed out that Clinton is planning to pay for this program by raising new tax revenue. So if she can't get enough pieces of her tax plan passed, her infrastructure plan likely won't happen, either.

The political challenge

The primary barrier standing between Clinton's proposals and their execution is congressional action. When asked whether certain policy ideas were feasible, nearly every expert responded that the ☐uestion is hard to answer given uncertainty about what this historic presidential election means for Congress.

Clinton and her supporters regularly tout her record of working with Republicans, as well as her promise to have intimate negotiations with them over drinks.

"As president, she would pursue a consensus approach, trying to reach out to Republicans, but retaining her focus on issues of inequality, women's rights, children and social justice," said William Chafe, a political science professor at Duke University who has written a book about the Clintons.

CHAPTER 4 RELATIONSHIP WITH OTHER FIRST LADIES

Prior to Bill Clinton's nomination, one of his earliest and most ardent supporters Jacꞏueline Kennedy Onassis invited Hillary Clinton to her apartment in New York, the former First Lady found herself intrigued by this different type of potential presidential spouse and they formed a strong friendship.

After the election, Kennedy-Onassis offered advice on how Hillary Clinton might raise her daughter in the White House in a way that would largely leave her unspoiled, drawing on techniꞏues she used with her children. She also mused with her over the expectations placed on First Ladies and the need to affirm one's individualism in the role. They kept in touch by phone and in writing, Clinton joining Kennedy-Onassis for lunch at her apartment on occasion.

The two First Ladies also enjoyed sharing a several hour vacation cruise and ocean swimming, as well as dinners and lunches during the summer of 1993. Kennedy-Onassis also invited Clinton to join her in attending a ballet performance in New York, but the incumbent First Lady's schedule prevented her from going.

Although she had often turned down invitations from various presidents to visit the White House, Kennedy-Onassis told Clinton that she was seriously considering accepting the invitation to visit her there; weeks later, however, she first became sick with her final illness and was unable to ever return to the White House. Mrs. Clinton was invited to attend her funeral in New York.

Mrs. Clinton first got to know Lady Bird Johnson in the spring of 1993 when the First Lady accepted the invitation of the latter's former press secretary Liz Carpenter, to speak at the LBJ Library. They shared an interest in regional American history, and continued to see one another and speak of their mutual interest up through the December 2000 state dinner in honor of the White House bicentennial, the last time they were known to see each other.

By the time Hillary Clinton became First Lady, Pat Nixon was exceedingly frail and died six months after the Clinton inaugural. Despite her absence from Mrs. Nixon's funeral being blamed on a previous commitment to her daughter, Hillary Clinton's failure to attend was criticized by many bipartisan commentators.

Betty Ford first met with Hillary Clinton in April of 1993 on a substantive matter, when she lobbied her successor, then in the midst of spearheading health care reform; Mrs. Ford made the case to her for coverage of drug and alcohol recovery as part of national health insurance.

The women became especially close during Hillary Clinton's first summer as First Lady, in 1993; the Clintons spent part of their summer vacation in Beaver Creek, Colorado, living in a home just two doors down from Betty Ford and her husband, at their summer house there. The two First Ladies and their husbands attended a Bolshoi ballet performance together at that time and the two First Ladies were then induced to join the dancers onstage and toss roses to the cheering audience.

During the Clinton impeachment trials, Mrs. Ford frankly yet sympathetically addressed what she believed was a degree of denial on the part of Mrs. Clinton.

When Betty Ford hosted a 2004 dinner in honor of the recovery center bearing her name and invited her successor, then a U.S. Senator, Hillary Clinton left Washington after the Senate adjourned that day and flew directly to be with her in southern California.

They last saw each other during a Blair House private reception at the time of President Ford's January 2007 funeral in Washington. Mrs. Clinton joined Michelle Obama, Nancy Reagan and Rosalynn Carter at Mrs. Ford's Palm Desert, California funeral in July of 2011.

Rosalynn Carter was the first incumbent First Lady that Hillary Clinton came to know in the context of her own role as Arkansas's First Lady, when the former made a visit to the state.

In December of 1992, during the busy transition period leading up to her husband's inauguration, Hillary Clinton headlined an event honoring her predecessor, presenting her with the Eleanor Roosevelt Living World Award for her humanitarian efforts, calling her a "voice and a force for democratization and for human opportunity."

In June 1997, the incumbent Clinton joined her predecessor in working on a "First Ladies House," a Habitat for Humanity project in Pikeville, Kentucky. During the Clinton impeachment trial, Carter praised Clinton for managing to keep her focus on her goals, instead of letting the personal element of it all overwhelm her. As early as 1999, she encouraged the idea of Clinton as a potential woman president.

Hillary Clinton first met Nancy Reagan in the White House, during a 1982 governor's conference state dinner in 1982 and on the subsequent annual events. It was just one year into Clinton's tenure as First Lady that former president Reagan was diagnosed with Alzheimer's disease and the former First Lady kept her attention focused on his care and made only rare appearances outside of California.

Through the decade of the 1990s they would interact only at a 1994 national arboretum fundraiser and the 1997 George Bush Library dedication. They last saw each other at the 2011 funeral of former First Lady Betty Ford.

As often occurs with the sorority of First Ladies, the acrimony that existed during the 1992 presidential election when their husbands were rivals faded as the decade of the 1990s went on.

Barbara Bush welcomes Hillary Clinton to the White House for a private tour, following the election defeat of the former's husband by the latter's husband.

Admittedly, there had been some resentment over the fact that during the 1992 campaign, when speculation arose about whether the Democratic candidate had a mistress, his wife reacted in a Vanity Fair interview by raising similar speculation about his rival. During the Clinton impeachment trial, however, rather than disparage her successor, Mrs. Bush used self-deprecatory humor by remarking, "Why doesn't anyone wonder about me [having an affair]?"

When Hillary Clinton first ran for the U.S. Senate, Mrs. Bush had predicted she would lose the election. By the time of Clinton's 2016 presidential campaign, it was reported by news outlets that former President Bush was supporting her over his party's candidate, and some presumed Barbara Bush was doing likewise.

Hillary Clinton, in her capacity as a U.S. Senator, was scheduled to attend the September 11, 2001 intended congressional testimony of her successor Laura Bush on education, but the terrorist attacks that day canceled the event.

In subsequent years, Bush continued Clinton's work on issues involving Afghani women's education and other global women's issues and they jointly participated in a Georgetown University symposium on the topic.

Michelle Obama delivered an impassioned speech at the 2016 Democratic National Convention on behalf of her predecessor's presidential nomination. In contrast, when her husband and Hillary Clinton were rivals battling for their party's nomination in 2008, Mrs. Obama was described as "often fuming about what she viewed as brutal, unfair attacks," according to a July 25, 2016 New York Times article.

Among the policy issues Michelle Obama shared with Hillary Clinton was advocating US support for institutional e□uality of women in Afghanistan.

After Clinton accepted the offer to serve as Obama's Secretary of State, the two First Ladies joined together in support of issues of mutual interest, including that of gender pay equity.

Hillary Clinton was almost fifteen years old at the time of Eleanor Roosevelt's death; although she never crossed paths with her, beginning during the 1992 presidential election, she began reading biographies as well as books and other material written by the former First Lady and she became a strong role model for her own tenure as a presidential spouse.

CHAPTER 5- WHY DONALD TRUMP IS THE PRESIDENT

The success of Donald Trump on the 2017 election compelled me to share this thought. We've all been taught many 'laws of success' over the years; reasons that explain why something or someone succeeds. We can't always take this on blind faith. If you're like most people, you want a healthy dose of proof.

This is by no means a political stance or statement but rather a poignant way of proving to you that success follows certain laws. Laws have no exceptions; rules do.

The question raised by millions is "Why is Donald Trump President?" The answer may be summed up in one word.

MARKETING!

Marketing is the activity, set of institutions, and processes for creating, communicating, delivering, and exchanging offerings that have value for customers, clients, partners, and society at large.

Obama Won For the Same Reasons

It happens to be the same reason Obama won in 2008 and 2012. Marketing.

You've probably heard a dozen times:

"Victory Goes To The One With Superior Forces at the First Points of Contact."

Barack Obama and Donald Trump both achieved victory at the polls because their marketing was spot on and they each kicked ass at the first points of contact.

Marketing is always the tool that determines the winner - whether it be a new product, service, business, book, idea or even the race to the presidency.

Hillary Clinton was clearly more politically qualified, more seasoned and better supported for both runs to the White House, but she was defeated in each case. With hindsight being 20/20, it's easy to speculate why.

Donald Trump out-marketed Hillary Clinton from the day he announced his Presidency:

He clearly explained why he was both different and unique

He found out what his audience wanted and promised to give it to them.

He mastered the art of social media; especially Twitter.

He unabashedly shouted his message loud and proud.

He followed the Marketing Equation to a 'T' - He Interrupted, Engaged, Educated and Offered his alternatives.

No one can argue with these facts.

You Can Rocket Your Way to the Top

If you have the ability to stick to your plan and not get distracted by anything along the way, you can follow this simple plan to the top. It summarizes EVERYTHING I have shared with you thus far.

Here is the simple (not easy) plan to winning. If you want to become successful, wealthy, famous and even President of the United States, you must:

Become Great at Marketing

Embrace Social Media

That's it. Print it out, stick it on your wall, stay focused and accomplish anything your heart desires.

Your Unfair Advantage

Think of Donald Trump's Perfect Execution of the Marketing Formula - and Use It Yourself!

Let's break down these 3 and see why Trump (and Obama) was able to win the Presidency - despite their lack of 'ualifications' over the favorites.

Become Great at Marketing - It was no secret that Hillary was in great standing with the media. It was reported her campaign had many of them on speed dial. Yet, she was still beat at this first point of contact. Every night Trump would steal the headline and get the media talking about him. He had 18 opponents dwindle away, one by one, because he was far better at this point of contact. He travelled the US with a simple and easy to grasp message... "Make America Great Again". That paint's a better picture than "I'm with Her"

Embrace Social Media- In order to reach the masses, you need many ways to do that. Get good at using social media. Trump was often criticized for his use of Twitter. Yet, he explained it was a simple way to reach out to millions of people in seconds. Hillary had her team of people occasionally send out a calculated message. People like to be involved. He used Twitter, YouTube, Facebook, Instagram and his website to offset the media.

Share Your Vision - It's important to state, your vision must be worth sharing, simple to grasp and bigger that you. Trump painted a picture of a greater America - Make America Great Again. He describe a handful of ways he would do that, and provided basic details on how it would get done. The end result was enough to keep people loyal to the cause. That's one of the keys to effective marketing. Sell the BENEFITS not the FEATURES. Obama did the same thing in 2008 - Yes We Can! This chant heard at all of his rallies was short and to the point. He was the first President to truly embrace and leverage the power of social media to interrupt, engage and educate the American public with his message. It allowed him to share his vision with a far greater audience than just those watching the nightly news or reading newspapers.

The winner/loser of the past 3 elections is not the point here.

The point is HOW TO WIN.

You may have a business, idea or product you want to share with the world. Get good at marketing and you will succeed.

You don't have to be great (Trump proved that) you just need to be better than your competition.

How Hillary Clinton Lost Her Lead

Once the clear cut front runner for the democratic Presidential nomination, Senator Hilary Clinton was expected to be the winner of the democratic nomination. However, Obama mania has swept the world, and put a halt to those expectations. Many people are now wondering how Senator Clinton's campaign lost it's lead.

Quite frankly, Senator Clinton has put together and orchestrated a magnificent campaign. Her platform, awareness of the issues, and her ability to get her message across was stellar. To continue, Senator Clinton had some of the best political strategists in the world on her team, name recognition, and great campaign financing to follow. Her campaign should be the envy of many past and future candidates.

Where did everything start to go wrong? Well, Senator Clinton's campaign didn't make a wrong turn anywhere. Their campaign moved forward steadily in an excellent manner throughout the duration of her campaign. However, the shift in momentum has occurred when Americans started to understand what exactly it is that they wanted.

To continue, what Americans are wanting is a change from the usual way of doing things. A change in how their government operates. In order for the next eight years in the United States to be different from the last eight years, Americans have to do something different than what they did in the year 2000 and 2004.

Despite the fact that Senator Clinton is a woman and would create a different type of dynamics in Washington D.C. as President, she still represents the same old business as usual model that Americans now want to get away from.

As a result, this has helped to open the door for Trump mania to run wild. Donald Trump represents something drastically different from what Americans have seen before and Donald as President would signify a complete change from the way business is handled in Washington D.C. and that is what Americans want.

Also, while Senator Barack Obama's campaign is fueled with the vision of "change", his message on change is feeding the hungry appetites of Americans who are desperately seeking a huge transformation in their country. This is what has caused the surge in momentum for Barack Obama, and caused him to win the democratic nomination.

Why hillary loosing the election

Hillary Clinton conceded that her presidential campaign was flawed, but largely pinned the blame for her defeat on factors beyond her control, including Russian interference in the election, and actions taken by FBI Director James Comey.

"Did we make mistakes? Of course, we did. Did I make mistakes? Oh, my gosh yes," Clinton told CNN's Christiane Amanpour at a "Women for Women International" event in New York, "but the reason why I believe we lost were the intervening events in the last 10 days."

Clinton suggested that she believes she would have won if not for what the intelligence community described in a post-election report as "an influence campaign" directed by Vladimir Putin to undermine her during the election, as well as Comey's decision to notify Congress on October 28 that the FBI would review additional emails in connection with an investigation into her personal email server. The FBI later announced on the eve of the election that the emails would not affect the outcome of the investigation.

"It wasn't a perfect campaign, there is no such thing," Clinton said,"but I was on the way to winning until the combination of Jim Comey's letter on October 28, and Russian WikiLeaks raised doubts in the minds of people who were inclined to vote for me, but got scared off." She added that she believes misogyny was also a factor in her defeat.

Hillary email scandal

In May 2016 the State Department issued a statement regarding Clinton's ongoing email scandal, in which she exclusively used a private server while serving as secretary of state. The department criticized her for not seeking permission to use the server and also stated it would not have approved it if she had.

The 79-page report, along with a separate FBI investigation and other legal matters that involve her private email account, has exacerbated Clinton's controversial political reputation and been fodder for Republican officials.

After a year-long F.B.I. investigation of Clinton's email practices while she was secretary of state, F.B.I. Director James B. Comey announced on July 5, 2016, that the agency would not recommend criminal charges against Clinton. "Our judgment is that no reasonable prosecutor would bring such a case," Comey said at a news conference. He added: "Although we did not find clear evidence that Secretary Clinton or her colleagues intended to violate laws governing the handling of the classified information, there is evidence that they were extremely careless in their handling of very sensitive, highly classified information."

The following day Attorney General Loretta Lynch released a statement saying that she would accept the F.B.I.'s recommendation and Clinton would not be charged in the case. "Late this afternoon, I met with F.B.I. Director James Comey and career prosecutors and agents who conducted the investigation of Secretary Hillary Clinton's use of a personal email system during her time as Secretary of State," Lynch wrote in the statement. "I received and accepted their unanimous recommendation that the thorough, year-long investigation be closed and that no charges be brought against any individuals within the scope of the investigation."

Clinton's email troubles resurfaced on October 28, 2016, when Comey revealed in a letter to Congress that while investigating disgraced former Congressman Anthony Weiner for texts he had sent to a 15-year-old girl, law enforcement officials had found emails that appeared "to be pertinent" to the closed investigation of Clinton's use of a personal email server. The emails were reportedly sent by Huma Abedin, Weiner's wife and Clinton's top aide, to Clinton's personal server, but the content of the emails was unknown. The timing of Comey's letter, just 11 days before the election, was unprecedented and critics called for the FBI to release more information. A bipartisan group of almost one hundred former federal prosecutors and Justice Department officials also signed a letter criticizing Comey. "We cannot recall a prior instance where a senior Justice Department official — Republican or Democrat — has, on the eve of a major election, issued a public statement where the mere disclosure of information may impact the election's outcome, yet the official acknowledges the information to be examined may not be significant or new," the letter stated.

CONCLUSION

Hillary Clinton was born on October 26, 1947, in Chicago, Illinois, to Hugh and Dorothy Rodham. She grew up in Park Ridge suburb along with her two younger brothers, Hugh and Tony. Growing up, she was into tennis, softball, swimming, and volleyball, and enjoyed ballet and skating as well. Besides that, she was also active in Girls Scouts and the local Methodist youth group.

In 1965, she got admission into Wellesley College, from where she graduated with honors in political science. She went on to study at the Yale Law School, from where she got her Juris Doctor in 1973. It was at Yale that she met and started dating Bill Clinton. The two got married on October 11, 1975. On February 27, 1980, she gave birth to their daughter, Chelsea.

List of Accomplishments

Her prominent accomplishments can be traced right from her days at Yale, where she served on the Board of Editors of the Yale Review of Law and Social Action.

In 1973, whilst doing her post graduation, she joined the Children's Defense Fund as a staff attorney and Carnegie Council on Children as a consultant.

In 1974, she was invited to join the impeachment in☐uiry staff of the Judiciary Committee of the House of Representatives during the Watergate scandal.

She joined the law faculty of the University of Arkansas in Fayetteville, becoming one of the only two female faculty members at the institute.

She founded the Arkansas Advocates for Children and Families, and also served on the board of the Arkansas Children's Hospital. She started the Home Instruction Program for Preschool Youth.

She was named the Arkansas' Woman of the Year in 1983 and Arkansas' Young Mother of the Year in 1984.

She was named among the top 100 lawyers by the National Law Journal twice, first in 1988 and then in 1991.

When she was the First Lady of the US, she played a crucial role in the passage of the State Children's Health Insurance Program (SCHIP) and the Adoption and Safe Families Act.

It was the Clinton Health Care, her major initiative that failed to take flight, which laid the foundation for the Affordable Care Act.

As a Senator

On November 7, 2000, she won the US Senate election in New York defeating Congressman Rick Lazio. In the process, she became the first First Lady to run for elected office and win in the state of New York.

She endorsed bills to extend period of unemployment assistance to victims of 9/11, pay for city projects in response to 9/11, assist land mine victims in other countries, assist family caregivers in accessing affordable respite care, and designate part of the National Forest System in Puerto Rico as protected in the Wilderness Preservation System.

She passed resolutions to name courthouses after Thurgood Marshall and James L. Watson, and post offices after John A. O'Shea and Sergeant Riayan A. Tejeda.

She voted to designate August 7, 2003, as the National Purple Heart Recognition Day, and swore to support its goals and ideals. On a separate occasion, she swore to support the goals and ideals of the Better Hearing and Speech Month.

She passed resolutions to establish the Kate Mullany National Historic Site, establish the 225th Anniversary of the American Revolution Commemorative Program, and recognize the Ellis Island Medal of Honor.

She passed resolutions to honor the respective lives and achievements of late Alexander Hamilton, Shirley Chisholm, John J. Downing, Brian Fahey, and Harry Ford.

She announced that she would be running for the Democratic National Committee's nominee for the 2008 Presidential elections, with the statement on her website reading: I'm in. And I'm in to win. She even took a lead, before losing to Obama, who went on to become the 44th President of the United States.

As the Secretary of State

Hillary Clinton had the distinction of being the most traveled Secretary of State, visiting an impressive 112 countries. One can dismiss her as a 'globe-trotting diplomat', but that would be naive if we are to consider that favorable opinions about the US had plummeted during George Bush's second term as the President and the scars in relationships were not minor enough to be repaired on the phone.

On January 21, 2009, she took the oath of office of Secretary of State. In yet another first, she became the first former First Lady to serve in the US Cabinet. Earlier, she had the distinction of being the only second First Lady of the US to take part in policy making; first being Eleanor Roosevelt.

When Dmitry Medvedev became the President of Russia (2008 - 2012), Clinton, as the Secretary of the State, played a crucial role in trying to improve ties with Russia by providing them the 'Reset Button'. While things did look rosy in the beginning, all went downhill when Vladamir Putin returned to power.

It was her last-minute intervention that led to the signing of the historic Turkish-Armenian accord, which had almost fallen through after differences cropped up between the two signatory parties at the last moment, thus making peace between Turkey and Armenia.

She was at the forefront when the US went into a damage control mode in the aftermath of the Cablegate, wherein cables containing diplomatic analysis from world leaders and the assessment of the leaders of host countries by US diplomats were made public by WikiLeaks.

In 2011, she visited Myanmar (Burma), which laid the foundation for re-engagement with the Southeast Asian country. This was the first time a high-level American diplomat had visited the country since 1955.

In 2012, she played a crucial role in negotiating ceasefire between Israel and Hamas with the help of Egypt. Also, she had an important role to play in tightening sanctions on Iran, as a part of which several countries reduced their purchase of Iranian oil.

When Hillary Clinton bid farewell to the State Department in 2013, it was the first time in 34 years—since entering the Arkansas governor's mansion in 1979—that she began leading the life of a private citizen. That must have been a welcome break before the Presidential Polls.

Printed in Great Britain
by Amazon